from head

Your body

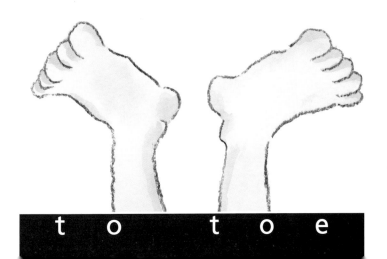

to toe

A **very** special **tiny** ball

Have you noticed how many things you can do with your body? You can run, laugh, play, draw... and so many other things that it can be fun to learn why. It all started when your mom and dad met. They loved each other so much that they decided to have you.

2

You were then inside your
mom's belly and you were as small
as a very tiny ball, so tiny, in fact,
that you would have fit inside
the dot of an i.

    Amazing, isn't it? But as days went
by, you grew and grew until finally
you were so big that your mom's
belly looked like a huge balloon!

3

You are so big!

After you spent nine months in your mom's belly, you were born!
Do you remember when you were a baby? You did not know how to do many
things back then. First you learned how to crawl on all fours, then you learned
to stand up and walk, and later you learned to eat by yourself. You have learned
how to do a lot of things since then, and you have also grown a lot!

4

And you still have to grow a lot more.
Growing up is fun, because you see
how your body changes as it grows.
It's a great adventure!

5

The body

The thickest part of your body is called the trunk, and your legs and arms come out of it. At the top of your trunk, your neck connects it with your head, where you have your eyes, ears, mouth, and a lot of hair that is sometimes hard to comb.

There are many different kinds of human bodies. There are people who are thin or fat, tall or short, whose hair is dark, blond, red, or brown. Wouldn't it be boring if everybody looked alike? We could not tell each other apart!

7

Look at those eyes!

You can see a lot of things with your eyes: colors, if it is dark or daylight, your friends, and the pictures in storybooks. When it is very dark, you cannot see anything.

A little scary, right?

You can also use your eyes to cry
when you are sad or you have hurt yourself.
Some people need to wear glasses
to see better. If they did not wear them,
everything would look blurry to them.
Do you wear glasses? You must look great!

9

Don't hide—I've heard you!

With your ears you can hear different sounds: people's voices, music, a train whistle... or your parents scolding you. You can also use your ears to know where sounds come from. If a friend calls your name, you can know where he is even when you cannot see him.

You can also use your ears
to hold your eyeglasses ...
or even earrings!

11

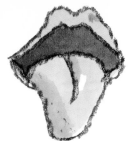

Stick out your tongue

How can you know what things taste like? Well, you can use your tongue
to find out if something tastes sweet, bitter, or sour.
You can find out what you like and what you do not like!
Your tongue is also useful to move your food around your mouth
while you are chewing it, or to make sounds ... or even to make faces!

12

What's that smell?

You can use your nose to smell flowers, food, people... or to blow when you have a cold! Noses can be big or small, wide or narrow. They can even have very funny shapes.

14

You feel like sneezing when dust
gets in your nose.
In fact, sneezing is the way to get rid
of the dust and to stop it
from going further inside.

15

Touch it, touch it!

Your skin covers all your body and you use it to feel hugs and kisses, hot or cold... and tickles! You use your skin to notice when others touch you or to find out what things feel like when you touch them.

There are objects that are very soft, like
a teddy bear. But there are things that are hard,
like the stubble on the chin of your dad or your
grandpa when they have not shaved.

17

Bones everywhere

Touch your hand. Can you feel the bones under the skin? They are hard, and you can also notice them if you squeeze your legs, your feet, or your head. Your bones and teeth are the strongest and hardest parts of your body.

18

If you did not have
bones in your body,
you could not stand up
and your body would
be shapeless,
like a puppet!

19

A mouth full of teeth

Your teeth are another hard part in your body. You use them to chew all your food into small pieces. When you were a little baby you did not have any teeth, so you could drink only your mom's milk or your bottle.

20

The first teeth to come out are called milk or baby teeth and they fall out when you are six or seven years old. But don't worry, they are replaced by other teeth that will last your whole life. You have to take good care of your teeth. You must brush them every day and you should not eat too many sweets. And don't crack nutshells with your teeth or they can break!

21

What did you eat today?

Do you know where food goes after you swallow it?
It goes to your stomach, which is a kind of bag,
but it really ends up reaching
every part of your body.

22

Your stomach is like a blending
machine. It stirs and stirs food
until it becomes all mashed up.
If you have chewed your food well,
your stomach will not have to work
too hard to transform it.

23

Breathe deeply

Where does the air go that you breathe? Put your hand on your chest and breathe in a lot of air. Now let it out. Can you feel your ribs moving up and down? When you breathe in, your lungs blow up like a balloon, and when you let the air go out, the balloon deflates!

When you are swimming under water,
you have to hold your breath,
but soon you feel you need to take in
some air and you have to come up
to the surface. Phew! That's better!

25

Are you hurt?

If you ever fall off your bike, and scratch your hands or knees badly, it will hurt and you will also be able to see your blood. This red liquid, which is a little sticky, travels all through your body as if it were a river.

26

Blood is so important that when you
have a little wound, a scab soon forms
over it to stop the bleeding.
Have you ever had
any scabs?

27

Take good care!

You have to take care of your body so it will work well. You should always keep it clean, eat the right food, do some exercise, and get enough sleep. Sometimes you don't feel well. Your belly aches, or you have a fever, or you have a rash on different parts of your body.

Doctors know your body very well. That's how they know what you have to do when you are sick—take medicine, stay in bed, or eat things you don't feel very much like eating. See? It's a good idea to take very good care of your body, because it is wonderful!

29

Activities

You're so big!

To check how much you are growing, you can mark your height on a door or somewhere else your parents will allow you to. Your birthday is a good day to do it. You can also glue a sheet of paper on a wall and ask friends and family to stand in front of it. Climb on a chair and use a pencil to mark everybody's height. Who is the tallest person? And the shortest?

The human body

Do you know the different parts of your body? Do you know what you are like? And what about your friends?

Sight

If you look through the bottom of a couple of drinking glasses, you will see things the way many people who need eyeglasses but do not wear them do. Isn't it difficult to walk without bumping into the furniture?

Hearing

Can you imagine a world without noise?
People who cannot hear use a special language
to communicate with others. They make signs
with their hands. Now you try it.
Using the signs in this illustration, you can try
to tell something to your friends.

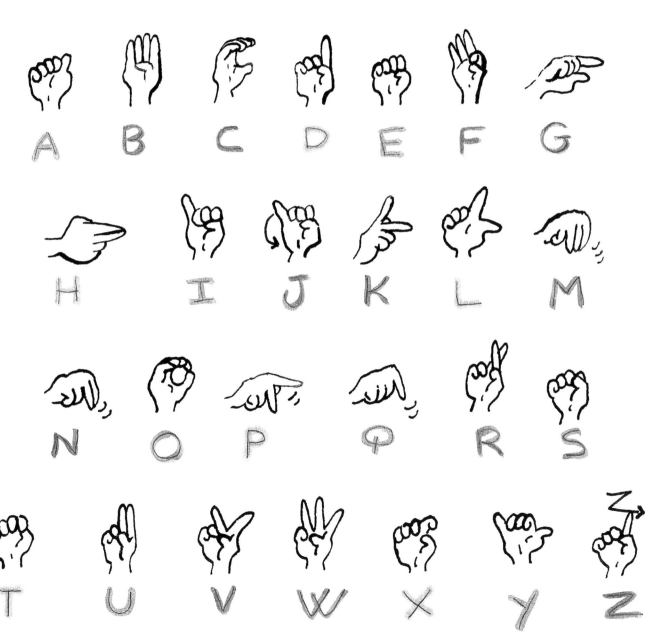

31

Smell

Did you know that many animals, such as dogs, recognize people by smelling them? See if you are able to recognize things. Ask your parents to cover your eyes and to place different things under your nose. Can you tell what they are by their smell?

Health

If you don't sleep long enough, you feel tired and cannot concentrate when you get up. At school you are in a bad mood and you can even get a headache.

A day is 24 hours long. How long do you sleep? Ask people you know what time they go to bed and what time they get up. Do they sleep longer than you do?

Touch

Cover your eyes again. Can you recognize things because of their shape? Touch them. Are they soft or rough? Smooth or wrinkled? How many have you guessed?

Bones

Trace this skeleton on a piece of oak tag or paper or make an enlarged photocopy of it. Ask an adult to help you cut out the different parts of the skeleton and staple them together. Good luck!

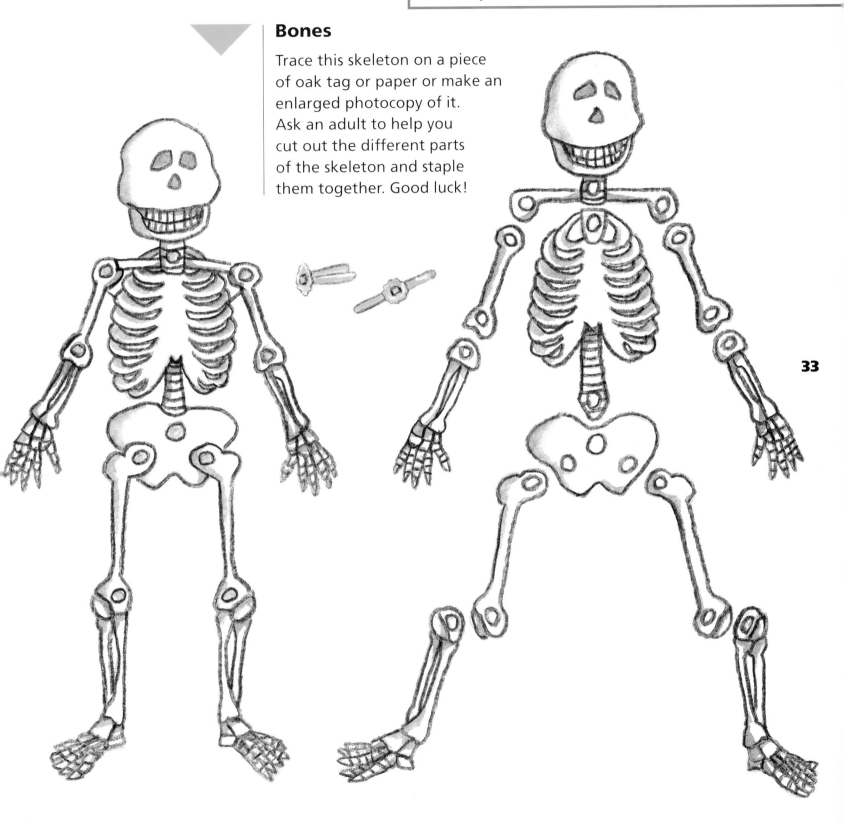

33

Guidelines for parents

A very special tiny ball

According to the child's questions, he/she can be told how Mom became pregnant or what happened when he/she was born. "When Mom and Dad first met, they realized they loved each other so much that they wanted to be very close together. They felt something so special that when they finally became very close, a lot of spermatozoa started flowing out of Dad's penis and swimming in Mom's vagina. Spermatozoa are like very tiny balls with a tail, and after they had swum for a long while, one of them met Mom's ovum and they stuck to each other. That's how you began, but you did not look like a baby yet; in fact you looked like a very tiny ball. But as days passed, your arms and legs were formed, and then your nose, fingers, nails, hair... until your whole body was formed and you were ready to be born. Mom and Dad were very anxious to see you after the nine months you spent in Mom's belly!" It is important that, whichever explanation is given, the child understands that he/she is the result of a union and that his/her body is formed by half his/her mom and dad.

What are you like?

You can tell the children about the five senses, relating them to the corresponding part of the body. In your head you have four of the five senses: sight, hearing, smell, and taste. Touch, which is the fifth sense, is spread all over your body. Through the senses you can perceive what is going on around you: the temperature, the taste of food, sounds ... everything that happens in the world. According to the child's age, you can introduce the concept of left and right, using the different parts of the body, traffic signs, and so on.

Look at those eyes!

You can use this part to play a game of moving around in a room with a blindfold over the eyes. According to the child's age, you can talk about the Braille system of characters made up of raised dots for blind people.

Don't hide—I've heard you!

You can try a game. The child wears earplugs or uses his/her fingers to block out sounds and tries to guess the words you say by looking at your lips. Use very simple words that the child knows well.

Touch it, touch it!

You can tell the children about the different colors of skin—dark, fair, reddish, yellowish—and how the color of the skin changes when it is exposed to the sun.

What did you eat today?

Some children may have problems eating certain kinds of food, so they can be told about the importance of a varied diet in order to be healthy.

Here is a short list that will enable you to relate food with activities or situations that are known to the child:

Milk, cheese, eggs, and almonds help your bones to be very strong.

Eggs, spinach, peas, asparagus, eggplant, and other vegetables make you grow a lot.

Fish also makes you grow and makes your skin and hair healthy. Cauliflower and beans also make your skin and hair look good.

Meat and clams are good for your blood.

Shellfish is very good for your teeth.

See? You should eat a little of everything so you can play, grow up, and become an adult.

Breathe deeply

While holding their breath, parents should count along with the child so he/she will keep the same rhythm. According to the child's age, it is a good opportunity for them to learn how to count or to start playing with a watch, learning to tell time, or talking about hours, minutes, and seconds.

Are you hurt?

According to the child's age, you can talk about the heart: "The heart is in charge of sending blood throughout the whole body. It pumps blood so hard that it can reach all parts in your body." The parent could have the child hear heartbeats by asking him/her to place an ear on somebody's chest.

Take good care!

Children can be told about the changing need for rest according to age.

We all have different sleeping needs that should be individually respected, but here is a list to begin:
Newborn babies, during their first weeks of life, may sleep 20 hours a day.
Children 1 - 2 years old, from 15 to 17 hours a day.
Children 3 - 4 years old, from 12 to 14 hours a day.
Children 5 - 9 years old, 9 -10 hours a day.
Children 9 - 12 years old, at least 8 hours a day.
Adults, about 8 hours a day.

As we grow older, we usually need to sleep fewer hours a day.

English language version published by Barron's
Educational Series, Inc., 2000

Original title of the book in Catalan: **EL MEU
COS DE CAP A PEUS**
©Copyright GEMSER PUBLICATIONS S.L., 2000
    Barcelona, Spain (World Rights)
    Author: Núria Roca
    Illustrator: Rosa Maria Curto
    Translation: Carlos Ganzinelli

All inquiries should be addressed to:
Barron's Educational Series, Inc.
250 Wireless Boulevard
Hauppauge, New York 11788
http://www.barronseduc.com

International Standard Book Number
0-7641-1518-9

Library of Congress Catalog Card. No. 00-190284

Printed in Spain
10 9 8 7 6 5 4 3 2 1